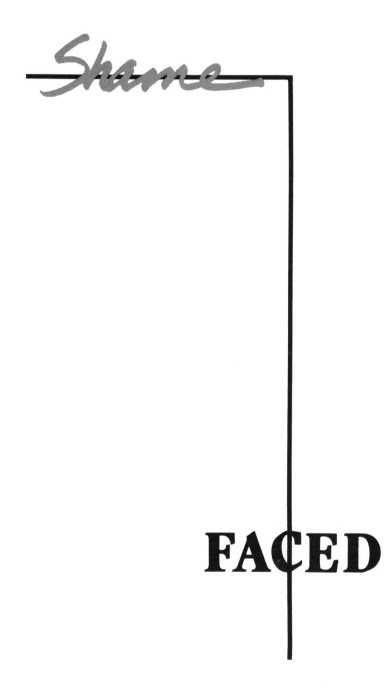

Shame

FACED

About the pamphlet:
Scratch the surface of most alcoholics or addicts and you will find shame. Even well into recovery, shame shackles us from growth and serenity. This booklet takes the reader onto the road of recovery through the Steps of A.A. With compassion and practicality, *Shame Faced* is filled with more than just awareness. It is filled with hope.

Stephanie E.

HAZELDEN®

INFORMATION & EDUCATIONAL SERVICES

FACED

First published March, 1986.

ISBN: 0-89486-358-4

Printed in the United States of America.

INTRODUCTION

Halfway There By Now

Shame and addiction are Siamese twins. One rarely exists without the other. You cannot find an addict without shame — or a shameful person without an addiction. Shame and addiction are attached at the heart, sharing the same blood that keeps them alive. Where one leads, the other must follow. Both exist behind walls of denial, growing like cancer, sucking out life. And both are destined to the same deadly spiral.

Shame's most important objective is *to not be exposed.* Most people who are "shame-based" don't know it. They can't. It's slippery. Sometimes it comes on so slowly, you won't know when you started to feel this way. And it is most often disguised as what it is *not:* irrational white rage, indifference, the overwhelming need to control, depression, confusion, flightiness, the obsession to use, numbness, panic, and the need to run. We will grasp whatever defense we can to survive slipping into the bottomless pit of shame.

Ironically, these very defenses saved us during our darkest moments. They may actually be the reasons we are alive today, and we can think of them as healthy reactions to very unhealthy circumstances. We can admire and respect ourselves for having them, before we lay them down and begin living a new life that no longer requires such reactions.

Most of us come into recovery as innocents. In the rawness of hitting bottom and accepting the First Step about powerlessness, we are like children, hoping everything will be fixed now. The reality is that getting sober merely gets us up to the starting gate. Eventually, if we are true to our recovery, we will collide with the feelings we ran from for years.

Recovery is not a destination. It is a journey. From the day we took our first sober steps, we began the lifelong journey toward serenity and, ultimately, love. The road is sometimes treacherous, sometimes glorious, and always unpredictable. It demands our entire participation, our full and total commitment from our core. But we cannot get there if we are shackled by shame. With shame running our lives, many of us will drink again, sadly concluding that "sobriety wasn't all it was cracked up to be." Many Al-Anons will stop going to meetings and slip right back into addiction because we can't imagine that anyone else has ever done the horrible things we've done when stone-cold sober. Many of us will never return from a slip because the shame devours us, and death seems to be the only way to relieve the pain. Anyone who has experienced the depths of shame can understand how suicide may seem to be a kinder solution.

But there is another way. The first step is to recognize our shame. Exposure is the only way out. If you are reading this booklet, you are already halfway home. The purpose of this booklet is to give you new hope and a few tools to combat shame. Shame may be a universal emotion, felt by all human beings because we can never live up to the perfection and ideals of our limitless imaginations. But it serves no purpose other than to kill us. This world would not be worse off without it.

SHAME — LIVING DEATH

Naked Exposure

Shame begins with feeling vulnerable and threatened. Out of control. Suddenly, we are exposed, and we are in danger of losing something, someone. When we are exposed against our will and our secrets are revealed, even before ourselves, we feel shame.

It can begin with a belief we formulated without even knowing it. Yet beliefs are not necessarily based on reality. They are, however, very real for us, personally. If we decided when we were very young that we were fools for loving a parent who left us, then it's possible to feel shame for the rest of our lives at the very thought of being left by someone.

And so, we work very hard at not being found out. For most human beings, loving is as instinctual as sleeping and eating. But for the shamed person, loving means being out of control. Frantically, we build elaborate defenses to make sure we are never found out. Never exposed. Imagine what that does to a relationship. There can be no intimacy when we will not reveal ourselves, not declare ourselves, not commit ourselves. That is the result of shame. Eventually, our partner will leave, frustrated and confused. And we will have what we so desperately tried to protect ourselves from: rejection.

Intimacy requires that we be vulnerable, out of control. The alcoholic personality has an aversion to being out of control. After all, didn't we drink to gain control over our feelings? Yet we cannot accept love without giving up control. In order to accept love we must sit still. We must be quiet. And we must open our hearts to someone else, who accepts us, in all our humanness.

It sounds wonderful. But for the shame-based person, it feels horrendous. Being loved means being exposed. And being exposed means being out of control. And being out of control means dying. . . .

The Cave-In

Shame and spirituality cannot exist at the same time. One cancels the other out. Shame separates us from others, from God, and from ourselves. It strangles our belief in a Higher Power. And without spirituality, we are profoundly alone in the world. How many times during our drinking careers did we really believe God had forgotten us? Even into sobriety, it is easy to slip back into controlling behavior for fear that God either isn't paying any attention to us, or doesn't know what He/She is doing. And if we are truly honest, we'll admit we don't always trust God.

To be ultimately, universally alone is so devastating that most human beings run from it. It is a phenomenon all people face at one time or another in their lives. It is part of the human condition. Facing ourselves, our own emptiness, our own humanness, is terrifying. Yet for those of us who have battled with shame, we fear we will never survive the confrontation.

The Paralysis

Shame demands that we *do* something, immediately, because survival is at stake for the shamed person. So it is understandable that we respond with a knee-jerk reaction. And so we become desperate slaves to our feelings of shame; jumping when we're commanded to jump, and losing all sense of self in the meantime.

These are the feelings of shame. They depict the process that strips us of everything we know about ourselves and the world. We may feel it only once in a while, or we may live in a constant prison of shame. The fact is that shame robs us of our personal growth, of spiritual consolation, and of relationships which die for lack of intimacy. We long for intimacy, yet have no way of accepting it. Like starving children who cannot keep food down, shame strips us of all the nutrients we need to be whole human beings. Shame keeps us from loving and from being loved by others. It makes spontaneity impossible because we are so self-conscious. And it seems to be the first step to giving up on life. We who know shame know it is possible to die from it. Why else would we run so hard and fast from it? Why else would we be so terrified? Why else would we abuse ourselves and others to avoid it?

Shame is simply the other side of intimacy, of acceptance, and ultimately, of spirituality.

OUT OF CONTROL

Somewhere, sometime, all of us in recovery have admitted to one fundamental shortcoming: that we were powerless over alcohol and that life for us was, indeed, unmanageable. In the First Step, A.A. encourages us to remember the desperate

4

groping for control of our drinking; how many times we promised ourselves: "Only one tonight," or "I don't think I'll drink/snort/shoot/smoke today." Then before we knew it, we were waking up in remorse, wondering why in God's name we couldn't use like normal people.

It took years for us to admit that our inability to control our chemical use was a serious problem. We fell short of the mark over and over, until we'd worn a path to hell. Our families tired of hearing the words, "I'll never do it again. . . ." But no matter how we tried, we could not keep our promises. We could not drink like normal people. Secretly, we thought we were deeply defective.

What few of us learn until we are very old and wise is that all human beings are born with shortcomings — everyone. And most people without addictions, who grow up in healthy families, learn to deal with this — even learn to laugh at themselves. Their sense of well-being comes from accepting themselves for *not* being perfect and from being accepted by their family for not being perfect. But in the chemically dependent family we could not afford to be imperfect. Very often, our minor mistakes were treated like felonies, and the punishment was often very shaming and abusive. And so, for most of our lives, and even into sobriety, we try and try to be perfect human beings, living perfect lives, doing everything perfectly.

It's our innocent, childlike belief in perfection that sets us up to fall into shame. As members of the human race we will always fall short of perfection. If someone had told us, when we were young and still forming our belief systems, that no one is perfect and that's okay, we probably wouldn't expect so much of ourselves. But since many of us learned to be loved by how perfect we could be, *not* being perfect meant *not* being loved. Or not being successful. Or not being a whole human being.

The Twelve Steps of A.A. teach us that to be human is to be limited. Not less. Not unlovable. Not bad. Just human.

We can never be perfect, or free of all character defects. We will always be working on them, for we strive for progress rather than perfection. When we strive for perfection, it is our shame trying to fortify us from ever having to be vulnerable.

Yet, acknowledging our shortcomings actually makes us more approachable — even more lovable. In A.A., we thrive on our differences as well as our similarities. This is how we nurture individuality. We work our own programs, and learn from people we never dreamed we'd listen to under other circumstances because they are so different from us. Yet they may have something of great importance to give us in that meeting. A.A. provides a safe environment where differences are tolerated, and where we learn to take responsibility, not someone else's inventory.

There is a temptation in being different. We all want to be unique. To call an alcoholic "moderate" can actually hurt his or her ego. Some of us actually think that being called "eccentric" is a compliment. But being different is a double-edged sword; "being unique" sets up walls that closed us in during our using days. We believed no one knew what we were going through, so we could talk to no one, ask no one for help. In sobriety we need to guard against these feelings that might keep us from sharing with our sponsor, or going to a meeting. Feeling unique can be one of the red flags going up when we're on a dry drunk or ready for a wet one.

Somewhere there is a balance between holding on to our individuality and knowing we are all alike inside, sharing the same feelings and problems in life. That is the beauty of A.A. We learn others feel the same things we feel. This is how we come to accept that we are really not alone.

Accepting a Power greater than ourselves in the Second Step brings us new strength.

*"Came to believe that a Power greater than ourselves
could restore us to sanity."**

The word *sanity* has its root in the Greek word, *to be
whole,* therefore the Second Step can be interpreted as the
beginning of becoming whole again. It brings us acceptance,
tolerance, and a Higher Power. In a moment of joy I can
look at my inventory and exclaim, "I am perfectly imperfect!" I can love myself for it. When I am depressed, however,
I can look at the same inventory and find evidence to prove,
beyond a shadow of a doubt, that I am not a worthwhile
human being. Not one of us *likes* being imperfect, but this is
the universal human condition.

The Second Step teaches us that our Higher Power plays an
active part in our lives as chemically dependent people, if
only we will allow it. After time in sobriety we learn the
effortless feeling of surrendering control over the outcome of
events. We hear over and over, "You are responsible for the
effort, not the outcome."

But at first, we have no idea what that means. Belly up?
Give up? Let other people do it for you? No. None of these
things. It comes from a growing sense of faith in our Higher
Power's abilities to work miracles in our lives. Eventually, the
second half of the Eleventh Step starts to make sense to us.

*". . . praying only for knowledge of His will for us and
the power to carry that out."*

This is where we come to understand the real meaning of
serenity: *Not the absence of problems, but the presence of
God.* We learn that the serenity of sobriety doesn't mean we
will someday be without problems. Serenity means we'll be
able to face life's problems with a sense of well-being we've
never had before. This comes effortlessly sometimes, and with
great effort other times. Why?

*See p. 25 for the Twelve Steps of Alcoholics Anonymous.

Perhaps it has to do with "control" versus "responsibility." To be controlling doesn't necessarily mean we are being responsible. We can rationalize that we're taking care of business, and if we don't do it, no one will. But this isn't being responsible in the truest sense of the word. To control means we'll go to any lengths to have things the way we want them. In doing so we have no faith in a Higher Power's presence in our lives. It is a lonely and desperate place. To be responsible, however, means we will do the work that needs to be done, without focusing our eyes on the outcome. It means accepting what we want and realizing what we need may not always be the same. It means showing up. It means consistency. It means accountability. And it means accepting the outcome as what is really best for us.

Controlling is a defense of shame. It is important to realize our defenses didn't go away when we laid down our drugs. On the contrary, defenses will often rear their ugly heads stronger than ever in recovery. It's part of the healing process.

Sometimes our character defects get worse right before they start getting better. So, we'll smoke more, eat more, shut down more, rage more. We will do anything in excess in order *not* to look at what is right on our heels. It's the chemically dependent person's first nature to run when there's trouble. It's our new second nature to turn around, square-shouldered, and face those damned devils that have haunted us all of our lives. Like any skill, it must be practiced before it comes naturally. For some it may come easily. For others it may take awhile. But then, God only gives us as much as we can handle. . . .

A.A. teaches us that being human means that even with our limitations, we can continue to dream of a better life. Hope is looking at tomorrow and knowing it will be even better than today. It is knowing God has wonderful things in mind for us, if only we will let Him have the steering wheel. And somehow, along the road of A.A., we learn that the only way to serenity is through acceptance of ourselves, as we are, now.

OPENING UP

To ask someone about his shame while he's experiencing it is like trying to discuss the nature of convulsions with an epileptic during a seizure. The very nature of shame is to protect itself from exposure. So opening up during a severe attack of shame may seem impossible for some of us. Thus we become slaves to shame, staying loyal to the feelings, and ultimately, just trying to survive. The end result is that we withdraw into ourselves and become untouchable, unreachable.

Ironically, defenses probably saved our lives in our earlier years. Many of us grew up in abusive homes with shaming parents, and our only means of survival was to isolate, through fighting, freezing, or fleeing. So we can look at shame as actually serving us at one time in our lives.

On the other side of that coin, however, shame also kept us from trusting anyone. Without trust we had no way of being loved. And without love, we had no food for our souls. So we spent most of our lives unnurtured. Many of us have feared we were incapable of letting others love us. To sit still and actually accept loving can make us feel terribly vulnerable. Sometimes tenderness feels more like a searing, hot bath than what the fairy tales promised. We can take only so much, and then it's time to withdraw again into ourselves where it is safe; where we have control over our world.

Because we're isolated we don't know we're not unique, weird, crazy, or bad. We don't allow others in. Instead, we can end up living in a world that borders on paranoia, thinking if anyone ever knew our real feelings they would also know how defective we are. We start accepting our brutal self-criticism as normal. We become so accustomed to pain and self-abuse that the next logical step is to use alcohol and other drugs to ease the pain, the fears, and the loneliness of shame.

THE SHAME SPIRAL

Shame often sneaks up on us when we least suspect it, and we think we'll never feel good again. In truth, however, the stage gets set. To be vulnerable to a "shame attack," we must already be hiding some feelings from ourselves. Understanding what happens before, during, and after an attack of shame is an important step in gaining freedom from it. Because shame is so illusive, so evasive, it is imperative we know the clues; particularly when we are first beginning to identify shame. After a while, we will be able to catch ourselves when we fall into shame, and deal with it before it takes another piece of our soul. But understanding is just the first step. It cannot take the place of action, which we will talk about later.

There are many theories about shame. From Freud to Sartre, from Nietzsche to Shakespeare, much has been said about shame. It is a mysterious and controversial feeling, which some argue is the essence of the human condition, and others believe is totally useless. Nonetheless, there is a method to the madness of shame. It follows a certain pattern, not unlike the downward spiral of addiction. Here is one description of the shame spiral.

1. The bond between us is broken.
2. I am exposed — I fear abandonment.
3. I widen the chasm because I go away to hide.
4. I abuse — myself, or others.
5. The one who shamed me, or who I think shamed me, tries to approach me.
6. I feel even more exposed.
7. I throw up my defense: fight, freeze, or flee. I get rageful, numb, controlling, perfectionistic, etc.
8. The shamer retreats in self-preservation and the chasm widens.
9. I feel abandoned. I was right. I am no good.
10. More shame, more isolation, more abandonment, ad nauseum.

What are the things we feel shameful about? Most often, they are so deeply buried it's hard to unearth them. "I am unlovable because my mother told me to go away," "Daddy left because I was a bad girl," "I'm inadequate because I couldn't get Daddy to stop drinking," are common feelings of shame from our past. Whatever "tape" you have, it still has the same effect. One small thing, an innocent joke from a colleague, a statement of fact from a friend, can hook right into that tape of ours and zap! We've fallen into the shame mire. Sometimes we don't even need an outside stimulus, we can hook into it with our own negative messages.

Getting an idea of what your tape is will give you protection later on. Eventually, you won't display your buttons so others can come along and push PLAY. And though we are only allowed limited control in this life, this is one area in which we can begin to take some control.

SHAME AND DEATH

Many of us have known shame since the cradle. Often we were "bad"; disciplined by having loving responses withheld as punishment. Some of us heard ridiculous things like, "No, I am not going to hold you because you're a bad girl." And so, being bad meant being abandoned. And in a child's small world, abandonment means death.

Shame and abandonment are closely related. Shame attaches itself to many situations and is different for each person. But almost always, when we peel away the layers of fear, abandonment is at the foundation of our shame.

If we are children of alcoholic or other shame-based families, we were abandoned. Rarely are alcoholic or codependent parents emotionally and spiritually present for their children. Most often they are too wrapped up in their own problems, trying to survive, and are unable to be available for their children. Abandonment may be as subtle as not being mentally present, or as obvious as a parent physically leaving the

11

child. But in the end, the results are the same. The fear of abandonment becomes indelibly imprinted on our personalities, often controlling us for the rest of our lives.

Over many years shame itself becomes an addiction born out of loss of control. It is compulsive and all-consuming like alcoholism. It creates such self-consciousness that all spontaneity is lost. It has a spiral, like chemical addiction. The more shame we feel, the easier it is to abuse ourselves or others and feel more shame.

Recovering from addiction is also recovery from shame because it brings with it a sense of well-being that we have never known. In *Alcoholics Anonymous,** pages 83 and 84, the promises of recovery are listed.

1. *We are going to know a new freedom and a new happiness.*
2. *We will not regret the past nor wish to shut the door on it.*
3. *We will comprehend the word serenity and we will know peace.*
4. *No matter how far down the scale we have gone, we will see how our experience can benefit others.*
5. *That feeling of uselessness and self-pity will disappear.*
6. *We will lose interest in selfish things and gain interest in our fellows.*
7. *Self-seeking will slip away.*
8. *Our whole attitude and outlook upon life will change.*
9. *Fear of people and of economic insecurity will leave us.*
10. *We will intuitively know how to handle situations which used to baffle us.*
11. *We will suddenly realize that God is doing for us what we could not do for ourselves.*

---

*Available through Hazelden.

It takes a belief in a Power greater than ourselves to enter recovery from addiction, so that we find the promises of A.A. coming true in our lives. One look at the Twelve Steps of A.A. reveals that seven of the Steps talk of work with our Higher Power. And as we walk the road of recovery from our addictions, we are simultaneously healing from the wounds of shame. The Twelve Step program is a simple solution for a very complex set of problems.

DOING VERSUS BEING

The Difference Between Guilt and Shame

As we mature in recovery we learn to define our varying emotions. In early recovery it's not unusual for emotions to be all mixed up; therefore we are unable to understand the subtle shadings between feelings. But it is important to recognize these differences so we can begin to take care of ourselves. We will never be without feelings, and we can't necessarily control them. But we learn in recovery that when we take responsibility we have more choices. Sometimes, choices we never dreamed we'd have.

Shame and guilt are two very different emotions. Guilt is the simplest to understand and recognize. It's an action emotion. It's the beginning of amends. It stems from doing something we know is wrong; like stealing, lying, or cheating. Guilt happens to us when we break clear, specific rules. And the degree of guilt we feel is equal to the crime. If I cheat at cards I will feel twinges of guilt. If I cheat on my spouse I will probably feel more than a twinge. To make things confusing, guilt and shame often exist over the same incident. If I cheat at cards I may feel guilt about the cheating, and shame that I am such a rat I would do anything to win. But these feelings can be independent of each other, too.

Shame is, as we've mentioned before, a more insidious chameleon, taking the form of everything it is not — rage, shutting down, controlling, depression, rigidness, numbness, etc. Sometimes we call embarrassment "shame." But people rarely commit suicide because they were embarrassed. No one likes being exposed, and that is about all that shame and embarrassment share in common.

Shame doesn't require that we *do* anything wrong. Shame is about our *being*. It isn't prompted by what we do, but rather by what we *are not*. "I'm no good at this game." "I'm so stupid." "I'm sorry I was so needy last night." Often, we're shamed by involuntary things. Someone doesn't love us to the same degree we love them. We showed up at a party inappropriately dressed. We could not keep a marriage together for our children. The core of shame is the lack of control we have. Shame surrounds that area of human existence where all human beings lack control, where human willpower is simply not enough. And where we fall short of the mark. Often, ironically, the more trivial the failure the deeper the shame.

The most simple way to distinguish between our guilt and our shame is to think of *guilt* as the feeling we get when we've broken a rule. Any rule. We know we shouldn't have done something. Then think of *shame* as not measuring up. Not meeting someone else's expectations of us. That someone could be as big as all of society or the man on the street. Shame charges us with being inadequate as a person. Shame comes when we feel we've fallen short of some imaginary mark set up to measure our worthiness as a person. It's usually a reaction far greater than the crime. And when we're consumed with shame we either fight, freeze, or flee, because our survival is at stake in our subconscious. That means we shut down, get overly busy, become rageful, go numb, become arrogant, or lie in a fetal position. Whatever defense we've constructed to survive, it keeps us unreachable and isolated.

It is important to respect our defenses, and not try to shame ourselves for having them. We do not need to complicate matters more. We will come out at the pace we need to. We know in our heart of hearts when we are willing to risk dropping a defense. And we must do it at our own pace. It only takes willingness. Our Higher Power will do the rest at the pace we can handle.

Being the imperfect perfectionists that we are as alcoholics, it isn't unusual to fall short of our own goals and expectations. This can continually reinforce our shame and keep us from gaining acceptance of our human sides, our flaws, and our strengths. And without acceptance, we cannot have serenity.

It's been said that guilt is: *I didn't do enough.* And shame is: *I am not enough.* Accepting that we can't do a thing about "not being enough" for someone else, is the beginning of recovery. We can accept ourselves as enough for us. This we have control of. In A.A. we learn that it is more than just "okay" to have shortcomings. We learn that grace is accepting ourselves as we are.

REGAINING DIGNITY

God, grant me the serenity
To accept the things I cannot change,
Courage to change the things I can,
And wisdom to know the difference.

The defenses we've learned while running from our shame have been self-preserving, desperate attempts to regain our dignity. Unfortunately, many of those behaviors have not worked to regain that dignity. Instead, we're frequently caught in self-abusive patterns with food, sex, or emotional binges. Like any other addiction, we promise ourselves we won't do it again. Then we do it again. Then we feel remorse. Then we punish ourselves more by continuing to do that which we're ashamed of doing. Regaining our dignity is a long process; not one that happens overnight, but one that will be our saving grace from the agony of shame.

The road to recovery from shame lies in the first five Steps of A.A.

15

Admitting powerlessness over our shame. This is very different from helplessness. When I am helpless, I have no choices. When I am helpless, I have no power and I have no hope. But when I admit powerlessness, I gain the freedom of choice back. Paradoxically, I begin to regain my power in the act of surrendering.

Believing that a Power greater than ourselves can restore us to sanity. Shame is very narcissistic. When we are in our shame, we are often grandiose enough to believe we are beyond hope. We are so focused on ourselves that we wouldn't be able to see a Higher Power if it reached out and shook our hand. Turning our eyes outward, to a source that we trust, a Power greater than ourselves, be it our A.A. group, an Al-Anon group, a sponsor, or a therapist, is a beginning of regaining hope. Later, it is the hope we gain from this leap of faith that will accompany us into the darkness ahead when we face our shame head-on.

Turning our will and our lives over to a Power greater than ourselves. Because shame is as slippery, as cunning, baffling, and powerful as our addiction, it is very important to not try and go it alone. In fact, if it were possible to recover from shame without help, we would have done it long ago. But since the nature of shame is to isolate us, we are hardly equipped to deal with it alone. Recovering from shame requires that we risk exposure. And we have every right to carefully choose the people we will expose ourselves to.

Making a fearless moral inventory. This is a very tricky Step for us: we can use it to beat ourselves up or we can use it to heal. It is important to do this Step after we've gained a spiritual base. In a fearless moral inventory, we look at our strengths as well as our character defects. It is important to look at each one of these with a goal in mind: to heal. If we think of these defects as the chains that keep us from spiritual freedom, rather than permanent limitations, we can more easily face our monsters. The importance of this Step comes in the exposure of our demons, for they are seldom as bad in the light of day as they are in the dark recesses of our minds. It is essential that we remove the shame from inside us, and put it outside where we can deal with it.

Admitting to God, to ourselves, and to another person the exact nature of our wrongs. The last step made us take the shame from inside and put it on the outside, in other words, expose it to ourselves. In this Step, we actually expose it to God and another person, so that we can be free of it. Admitting it to ourselves is not enough. We are too vulnerable to the power of shame. So finding someone who is trained in receiving Fifth Steps is essential. It is okay to interview this person first, to see if you feel you can trust him or her. Be overly protective of yourself, the way you would be if you were in charge of the welfare of a battered child. You are that battered child. And you deserve a nonshaming Fifth Step experience.

These five Steps are the beginning of a very important move away from the self-degradation that keeps us from serenity in sobriety. Looking to God, to our sponsors, or to a therapist, are some of the ways we can begin to become whole again.

Each day we can apply the principles of A.A. and Al-Anon to our shame. "Just for today, I will. . . ." And each day we can attempt to do just one thing differently. For each time we do something differently, we are one step farther away from the shame that threatens our sobriety, serenity, and spiritual growth.

Rule: Be Gentle With Yourself

Many of us have been brutal with ourselves. Perfectionism is yet another one of the hooks that can snag us back into shame. Gentleness with ourselves is one of the first steps in healing. This may mean giving ourselves a wide berth when it comes to making mistakes. We may repeat the same behavior over and over again, even though we don't intend to. It's important to remember that even when we seem to regress, it is only our unique way of going forward. Think of each act, both positive and negative, as a way our Higher Power has arranged for us to heal. As we start to develop self-forgiveness, we may have to do it over and over until we get it right. I had to think of myself as the four-year-old who had been emotionally wounded. I literally thought of her as my own child, imagining how I would treat her if she were in such pain. I imagined how I would support her when she was taking some very scary risks. I even imagined myself holding her when she was hurt or scared.

To this day she is real to me. Perhaps she will always be real. But the important thing is that she was the way I could begin to be gentle with myself. She was the beginning of self-forgiveness. When I didn't do things perfectly, when I failed at my attempts to pull out of shame, I began to forgive myself and try again. This was a major shift in behavior for me. Making mistakes had meant failure and rejection. In my family, if you made a mistake, you were shamed and there was no way out. I can't tell you what a relief it is now to be able to make mistakes and accept myself anyway. Today I am much more productive, and I have fewer problems taking risks.

Al-Anon

When I hurt badly enough, I was finally able to accept the gift of Al-Anon. Many people in Al-Anon are intimately acquainted with shame. And Al-Anon offers one more way to heal by the mutual sharing of problems related to shame. As in our recovery from chemicals, we must not isolate ourselves. We need to be told the things we forget when we need them most, like *Easy Does It, One Day at a Time, First Things First,* and, *This Too Shall Pass.* We need to know that others have been in the same pain, have done the same things, and are living full and whole lives in recovery. Al-Anon is a lovely, safe place to begin the healing process.

Therapy

It's important to consider therapy for shame; a therapist trained in recovery from shame can be very helpful. My therapist played a vital role in my recovery. I needed someone with whom I could build a relationship, risk exposure, and ask for reassurance in a healthy way. It was a chance to be parented the right way, and to learn to trust someone completely. And it was important that she kept the big picture in mind for me because I lost track of anything outside of my own immediate surroundings. Therapy may not be the only way, but it worked for me.

WAYS TO COMBAT SHAME

There are concrete things to do to get out of shame and regain hope. We can choose to listen to new messages. Just reading this book is a way of finding new and different messages.

The next few suggestions are immediate ways of dealing with shame. They do not represent an alternative to therapy. Recovery is a complicated and sometimes long process, and it doesn't matter where you start — it's just important to start somewhere.

Getting a Shame Sponsor

If you are in a Twelve Step program, you know about sponsorship. Chances are, too, that if you are shame-based, you probably don't have a sponsor, or you probably don't use the one you have. When it comes to choosing a shame sponsor, you can apply the same rules you have followed in A.A.

First, choose someone who has worked on shame and is further along than you are — someone who has something you want. This person doesn't have to be like you, but should be someone you feel comfortable moving through your discomfort with. Pay attention to your inner feelings about trustworthiness. If you don't trust someone for some reason, don't try to talk yourself out of this gut reaction. Instead, look for someone with whom you don't have to struggle.

It is also recommended that we choose a sponsor of the same sex. We might get distracted by issues that are bound to arise when we're dealing with the opposite sex, particularly when it comes to shame.

The next step is to use your sponsor. Many of us have gone as far as asking someone to be our sponsor, and then we never showed our faces at that meeting again. Remember, recovery from shame means risking exposure. We begin to heal when we see that people will not cringe and turn away when they see the real us. Instead, as we let people in, we will begin to learn how lovable we really are. A simple nod from others that lets us know they've been there, too, can be the beginning of freedom from our shame.

Doing a First Step On Shame

When we first got sober, admitting our powerlessness and acknowledging the ways our lives had become unmanageable were very important steps to our recovery. Painful as it was, our decision to turn our will and lives over to a Higher Power was reinforced by our acceptance of the First Step. We allowed a spiritual experience to happen to us. We surrendered in order to win.

The same is true of our shame. Looking at the various ways we have allowed shame to control us will give us the opportunity to be active players in our lives. Learning about our unmanageability sharpens our intuition and wisdom.

Affirmations

For most of our lives negative, self-defeating messages were the only ones we heard. We learned to carry forth the messages we heard as children into adulthood. Beating up on ourselves has become a habit we need to break. And so, affirming we're okay on a daily basis is more than just a luxury. It's vital.

If you are at all attached to your shame you will probably be embarrassed, at first, by these affirmations. But a sense of humor helps, and do remember to be gentle with yourself as you're learning.

These affirmations are very helpful in changing the messages you give to yourself. They are guides; not the gospel. You can make up your own as you go along.

I am a child of God and I deserve love, peace, prosperity, and serenity.

I am loved because I deserve love.

I forgive myself for hurting myself and others.

I forgive myself for letting others hurt me.

I forgive myself for accepting sex when I wanted love.

I am willing to accept love.

I am not alone. I am one with God and the universe.

I am whole and good.

I am innocent and totally deserving of love unconditionally.

I am capable of changing.

Just for today, I will respect my own and others' boundaries.

Just for today, I will be vulnerable with someone I trust.

Just for today, I will take one compliment and hold it in my heart for more than just a fleeting moment. I will let it nurture me.

Just for today, I will act in a way that I would admire in someone else.

Repeating these affirmations can be a strong reinforcement of our inner selves. Writing them daily, in a journal, is helpful. And, down the road, we can look back and see how far we've come.

SPIRITUALITY

**It is the wounded oyster that
mends itself with pearl. . . .**
Ralph Waldo Emerson

Spirituality and shame cannot exist side by side. Shame
separates us from our three most important connections in
recovery — ourselves, others, and God. And as long as we are
separate we will feel the terror of true aloneness.

Recovering from shame means that we have to regain
confidence in our Higher Power. It means that we come to
believe in our hearts that we are deserving children of that
Higher Power, who only wants the best for us. Most of us
have felt abandoned, even by God, and repairing that relationship can make all the difference in our recovery. Taking
the Third Step on shame, believing that God would like to
relieve us of that debilitating emotion, and then turning it
over to Him, is one important way we can free ourselves.

Imagine a happy life, a life of serenity and love. It's important for us to believe we can have this in order for it to
become a reality. And somehow, somewhere, it will begin to
make sense to us. Perhaps no one suffers without a reason —
not a punishing reason, but a healing reason. Even those who
are incapable of being honest with themselves teach us very
important lessons. No alcoholic has ever died in vain. Because, somewhere, one of us woke up and recovered as a
result.

We can take comfort in knowing our pain is not an exercise
in self-mutilation, but rather part of the healing process. Not
a day goes by that I can't look back, and know I am a better
person for having had hardships. I wish them on no one, and
I wouldn't want to face them again. But I am stronger now,
having survived and recovered, for I know today I have more
choices than I ever dreamed of. And hopefully, someday, I
can help someone else who needs a little hope.

Putting Will In Its Place

Sometimes life seems so easy, like riding a bike downhill. And other times it seems like we're stuck in a swamp. When our will and God's are in concert, life is wonderful. Understanding which "will" to turn over is one of the mysteries every alcoholic would like to unravel. And perhaps it is as simple as "my will" versus "God's will." Only when we are ready do we get the benefit of God's will for us.

The belief that alcoholics have no willpower is a laughable myth. It took great will to hide our addictions, to continue working through years of morning hangovers. How else would we have been able to survive the horrendous situations of our drinking days? It is not will we are lacking; it is the ability to know the difference between our will and God's will. It is through the Twelve Steps of A.A., the warmth and safety of our meetings, and the Serenity Prayer that we learn what we *can* control. And then, one day, suddenly, it all makes sense. . . .

I Can Will. . . .

Knowledge, but not wisdom.
Submission, but not surrender.
Meekness, but not humility.
Nearness, but not love.
Religiosity, but not faith.
Reading, but not understanding.
Congratulations, but not admiration.
Bravado, but not courage.
Dryness, but not sobriety.*

---

*The ideas represented here come from the book, *Lying, Despair, Jealousy, Envy, Sex, Suicide, Drugs, and the Good Life,* by Leslie H. Farber. Copyright 1976 by Basic Books, Inc, NY.

And one day, we realize the promises of A.A. have come true. For recovery from shame is recovery from our addictions; it is freedom from the prison walls that keep us from living our lives to the fullest, and loving our loved ones to the limits of our hearts.

There is hope. We should never give up on hope.

The Twelve Steps to recovery are as follows:

1. We admitted we were powerless over alcohol — that our lives had become unmanageable.

2. Came to believe that a Power greater than ourselves could restore us to sanity.

3. Made a decision to turn our will and our lives over to the care of God *as we understood Him.*

4. Made a searching and fearless moral inventory of ourselves.

5. Admitted to God, to ourselves, and to another human being the exact nature of our wrongs.

6. Were entirely ready to have God remove all these defects of character.

7. Humbly asked Him to remove our shortcomings.

8. Made a list of all persons we had harmed, and became willing to make amends to them all.

9. Made direct amends to such people wherever possible, except when to do so would injure them or others.

10. Continued to take personal inventory and when we were wrong promptly admitted it.

11. Sought through prayer and meditation to improve our conscious contact with God *as we understood Him,* praying only for knowledge of His will for us and the power to carry that out.

12. Having had a spiritual awakening as the result of these Steps, we tried to carry this message to alcoholics, and to practice these principles in all our affairs.

---

*The Twelve Steps reprinted with permission of A.A. World Services, Inc.

HAZELDEN INFORMATION AND EDUCATIONAL SERVICES is a division of the Hazelden Foundation, a not-for-profit organization. Since 1949, Hazelden has been a leader in promoting the dignity and treatment of people afflicted with the disease of chemical dependency.

The mission of the foundation is to improve the quality of life for individuals, families, and communities by providing a national continuum of information, education, and recovery services that are widely accessible; to advance the field through research and training; and to improve our quality and effectiveness through continuous improvement and innovation.

Stemming from that, the mission of this division is to provide quality information and support to people wherever they may be in their personal journey—from education and early intervention, through treatment and recovery, to personal and spiritual growth.

Although our treatment programs do not necessarily use everything Hazelden publishes, our bibliotherapeutic materials support our mission and the Twelve Step philosophy upon which it is based. We encourage your comments and feedback.

The headquarters of the Hazelden Foundation are in Center City, Minnesota. Additional treatment facilities are located in Chicago, Illinois; New York, New York; Plymouth, Minnesota; St. Paul, Minnesota; and West Palm Beach, Florida. At these sites, we provide a continuum of care for men and women of all ages. Our Plymouth facility is designed specifically for youth and families.

For more information on Hazelden, please call **1-800-257-7800**. Or you may access our World Wide Web site on the Internet at **http://www.hazelden.org**.